Freddie and his Cats

The story of a legendary rock star and his fabulous felines

Kitty Wilson

All rights reserved. No part of this book may be reproduced or used in any manner without written permission of the author.

Copyright © 2024 Kitty Wilson

First edition March 2024

ISBN - 9798883552679

Instagram / Facebook - Kitty Wilson Books

Dedication

To Dave and Isla, my technical advisors, proof-readers, tea makers and wonderful people, my parents, the best cheerleaders a girl could have, and the fabulous felines who 'help' write every book.

(If you spot a typo, it was them – not me!)

In a town filled with music and magic, there lived the legendary musician Freddie Mercury and his fabulous feline friends.

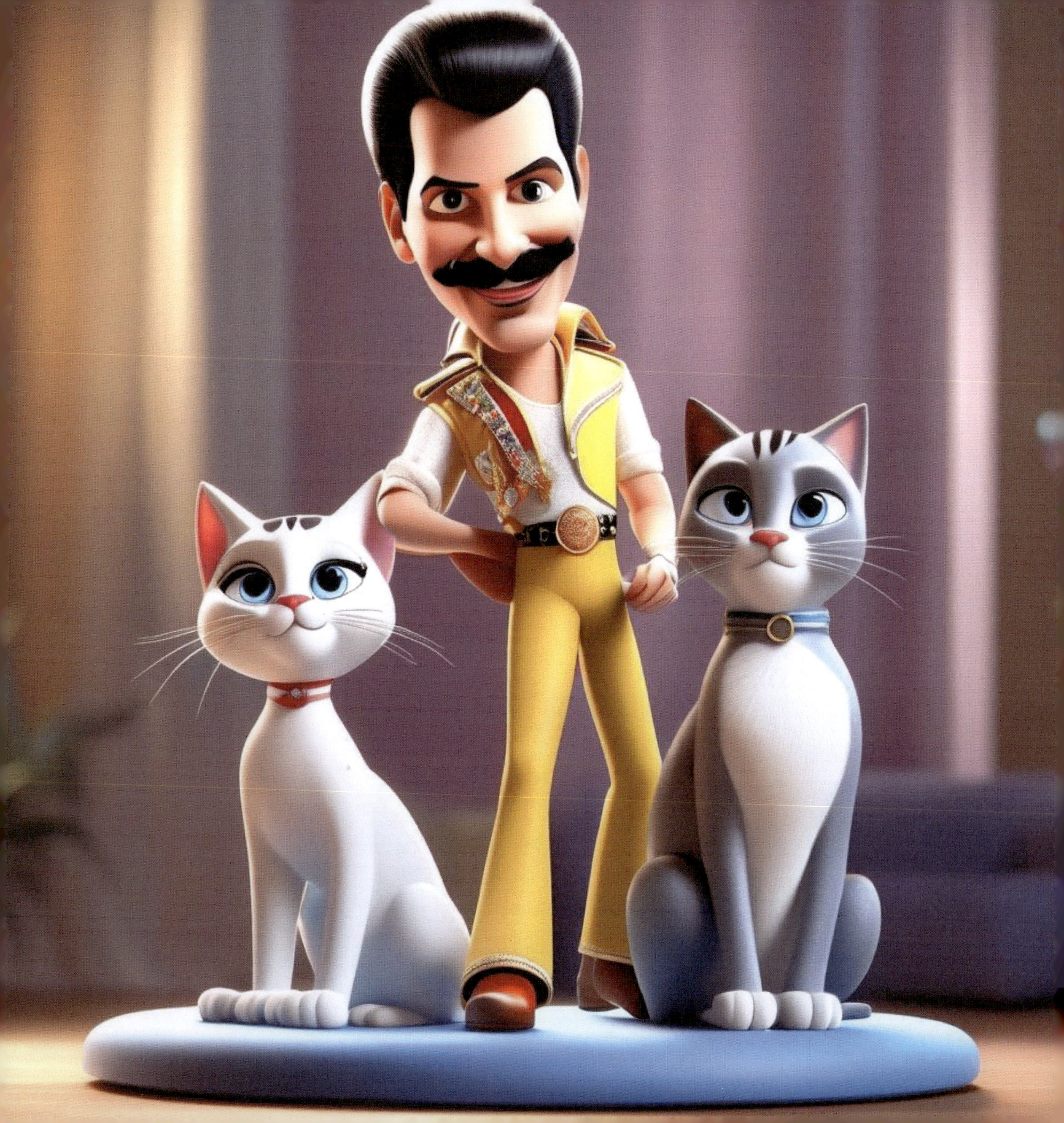

Freddie's home was a symphony of colours and melodies, with guitars strumming, pianos playing and cat paws tapping to the beat.

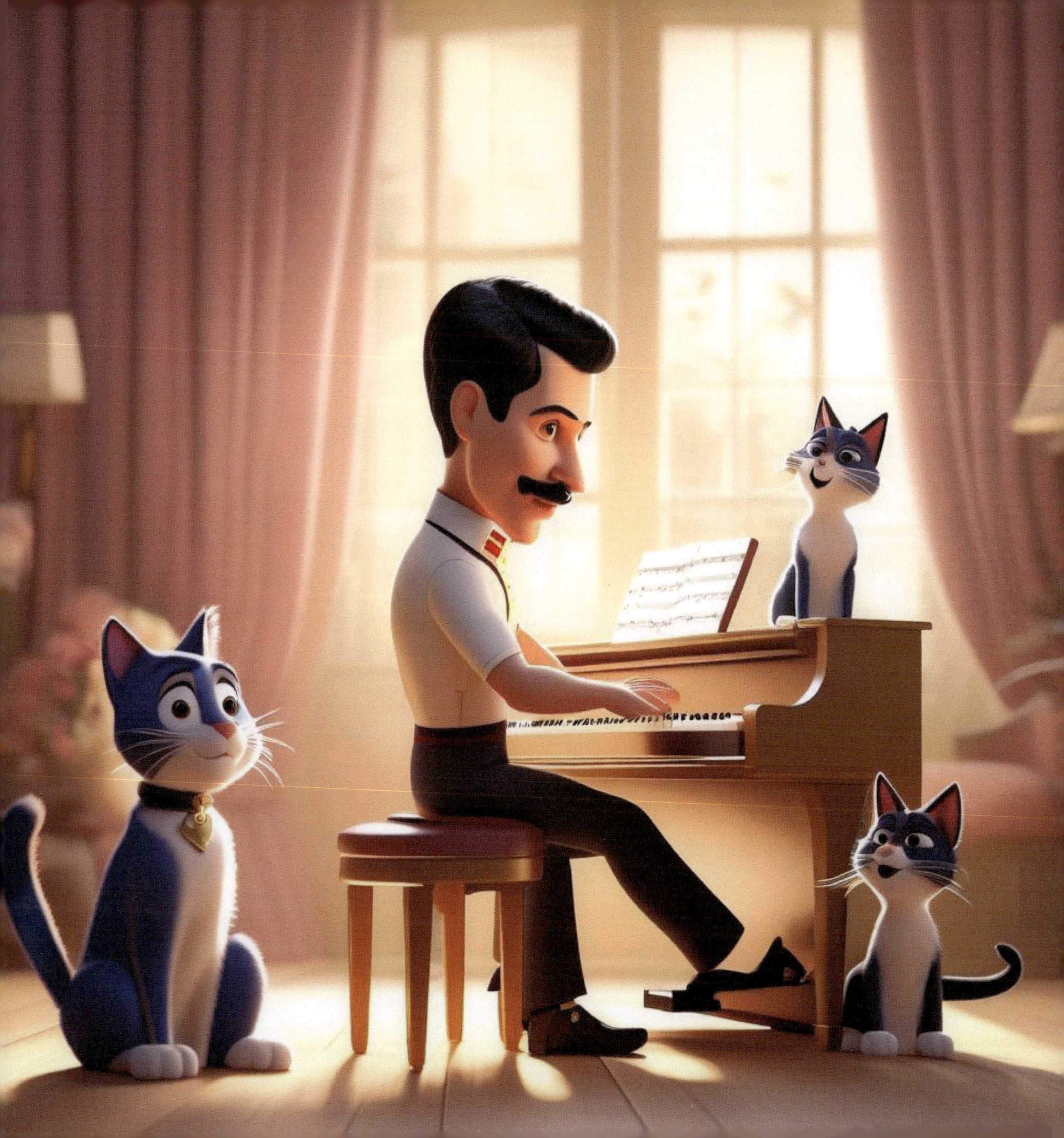

But what made Freddie's home truly special, was his 10 cats!

The cats were called Tom and Jerry, Tiffany, Dorothy, Delilah, Goliath, Lily, Miko, Oscar and Romeo.

All different shapes and sizes, but all special and all equally loved.

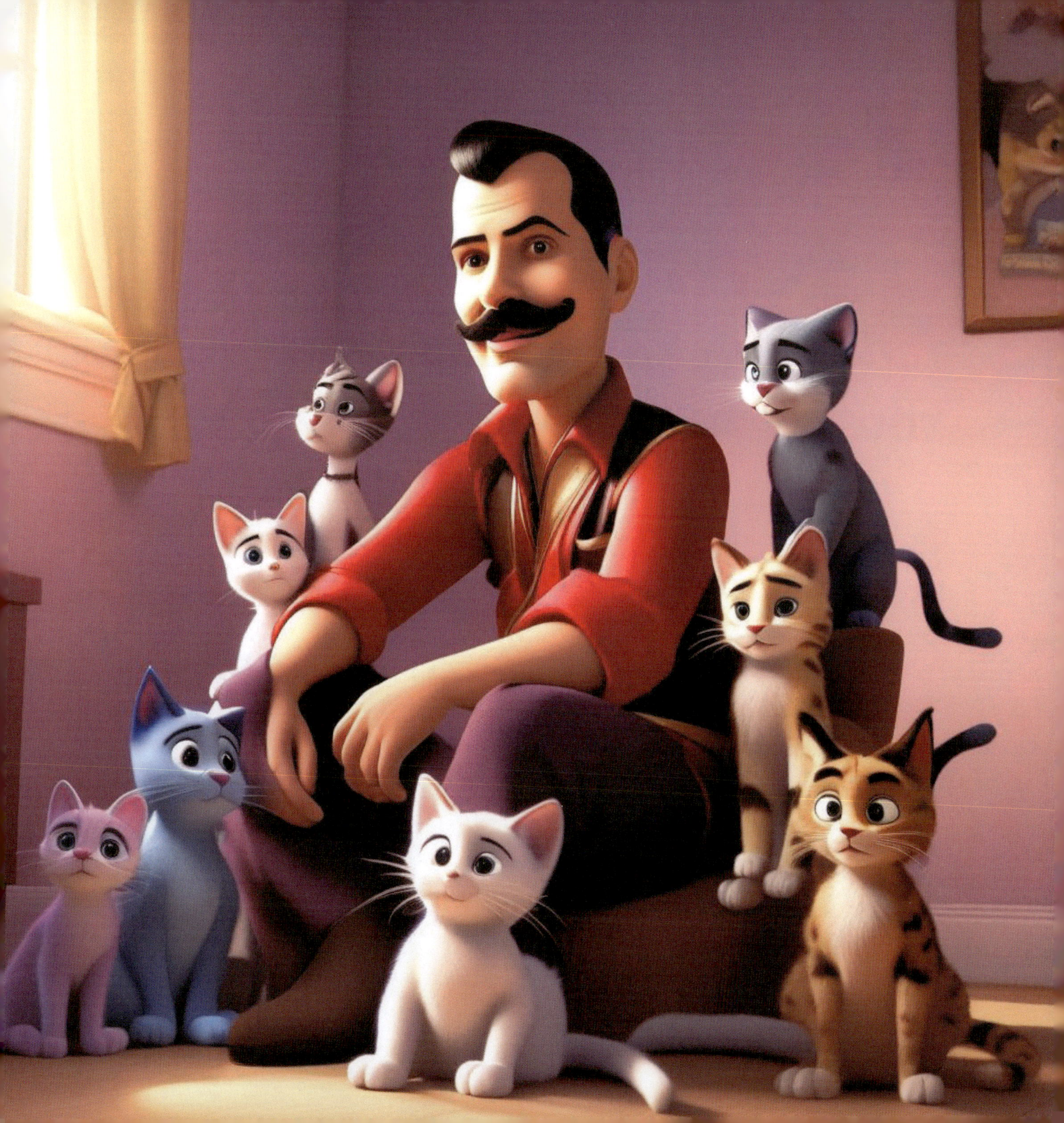

Freddie loved his cats so much, that they had their very own bedroom.

It was adorned with plush beds, scratching posts, and a cozy corner for purr-fect catnaps.

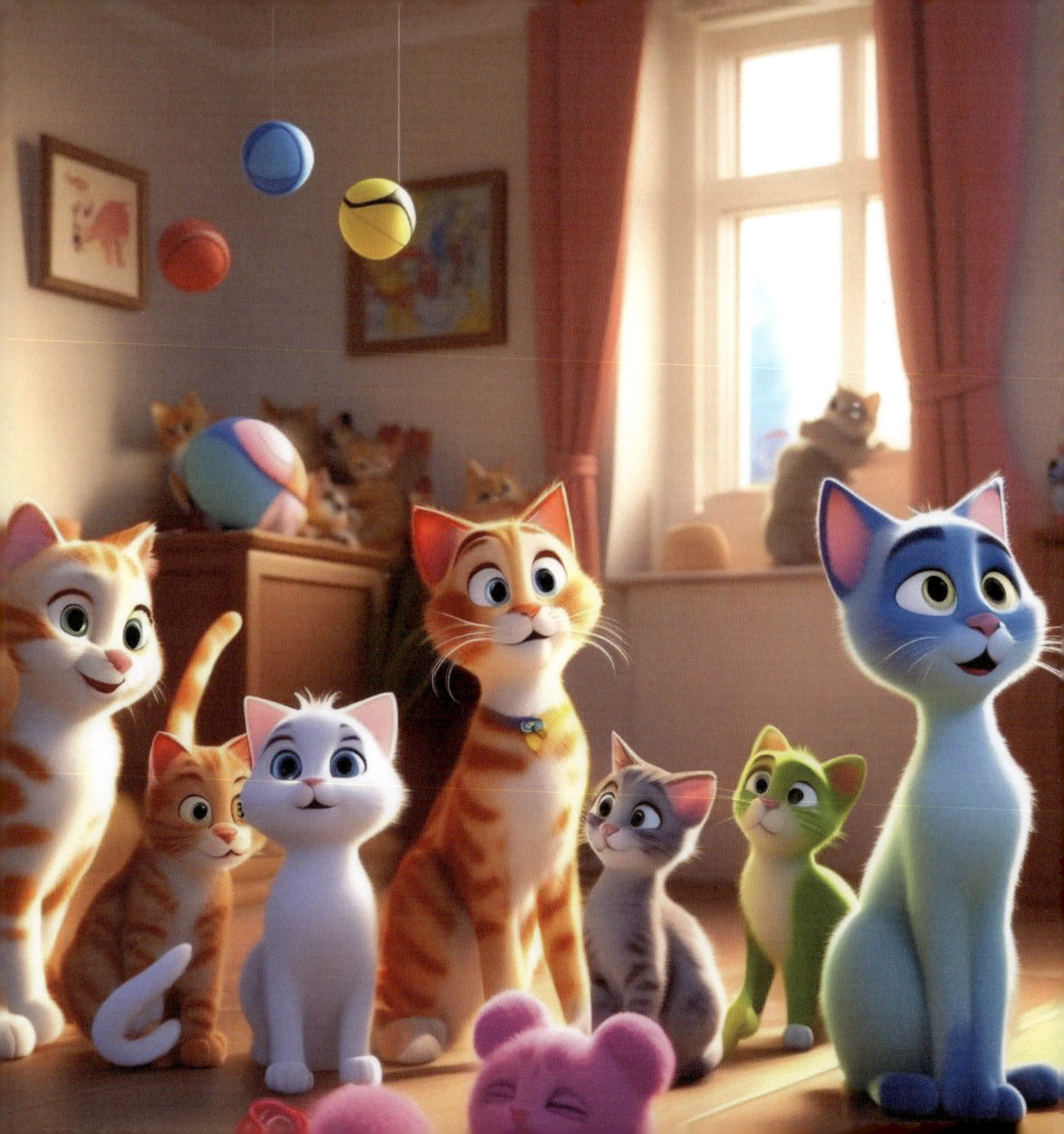

The cats had a kingdom of their own, where they could dream to the rhythm of Freddie's timeless tunes.

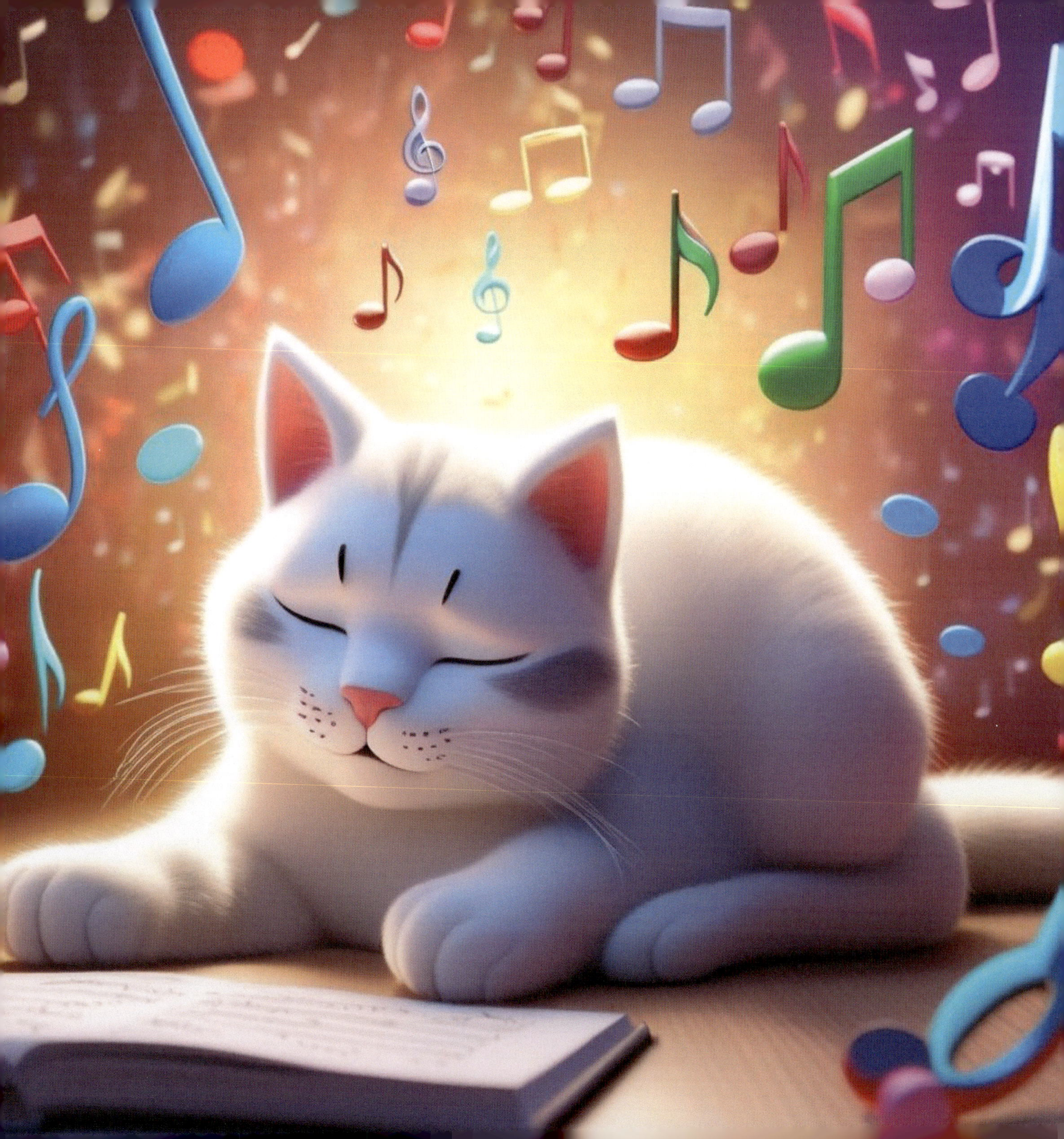

Now, Freddie was a globetrotter, touring the world with his rock band Queen.

But even when he was miles away, he found a way to stay close to his feline companions...

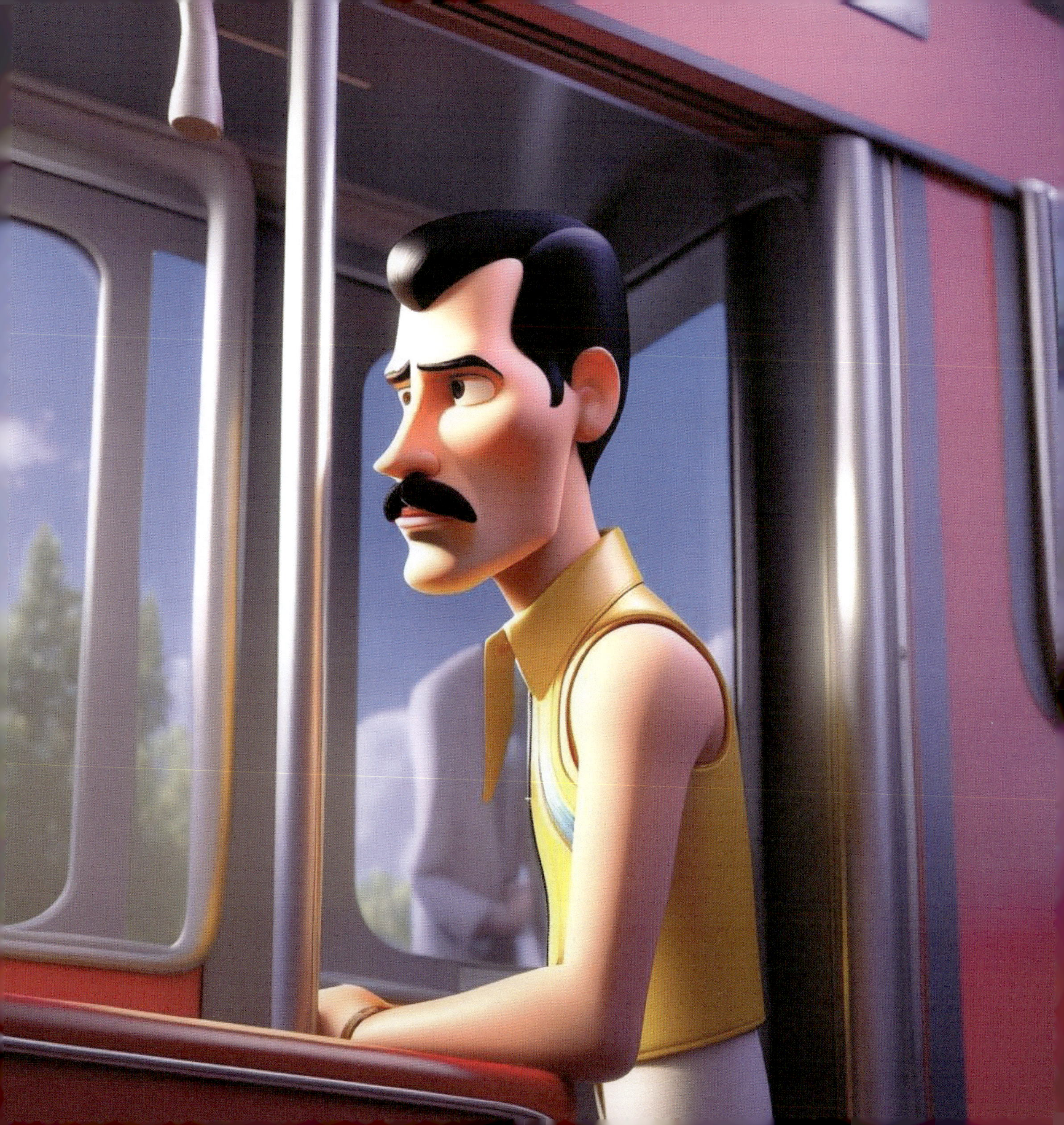

Freddie would pick up the phone and dial the number to the cats' room, just to hear their happy purrs and share tales of his adventures on the road.

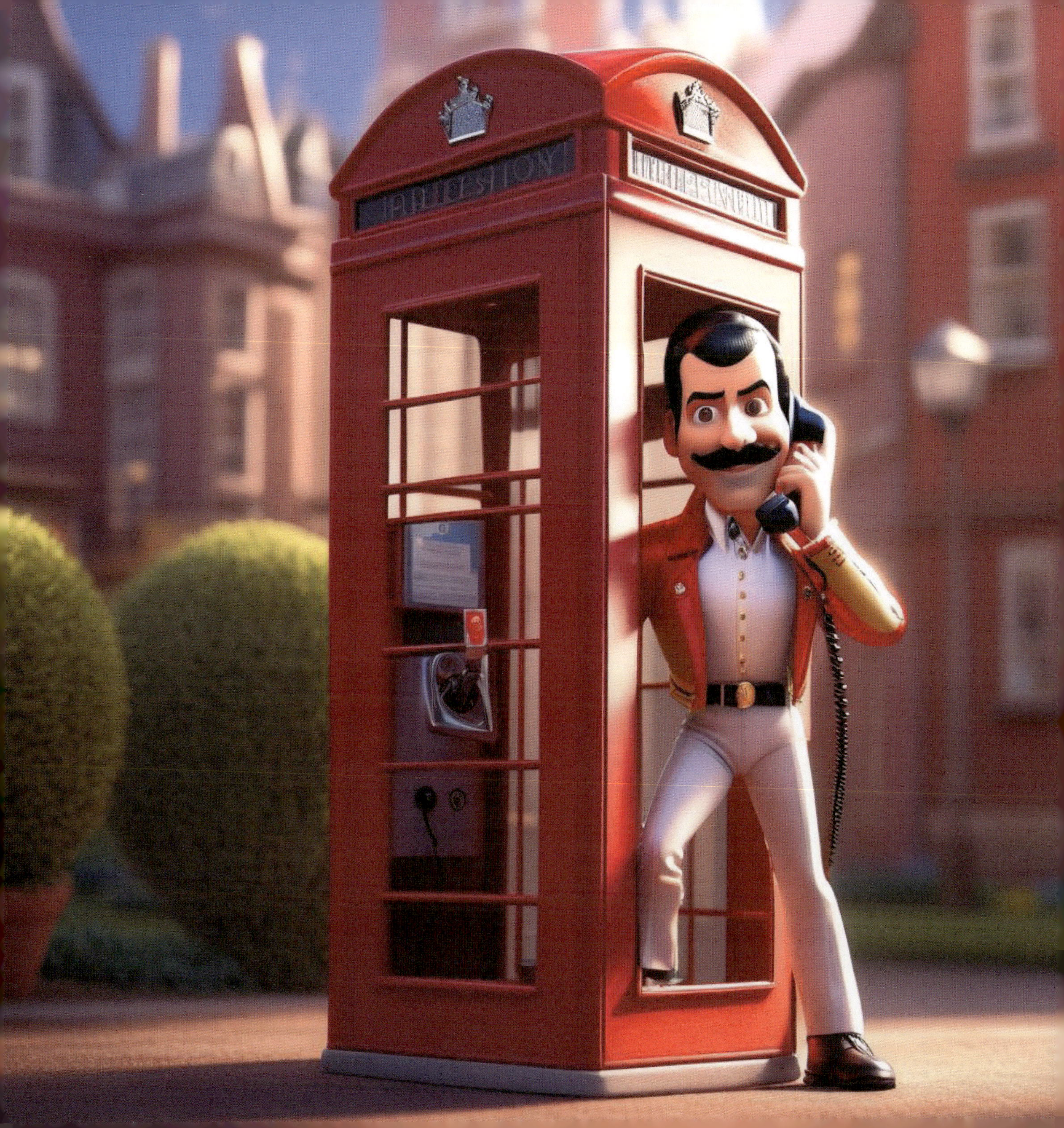

"Hello, my fabulous felines!" Freddie would sing into the phone.
"How are you today?"
The cats would respond with delighted meows, as if they understood every word.

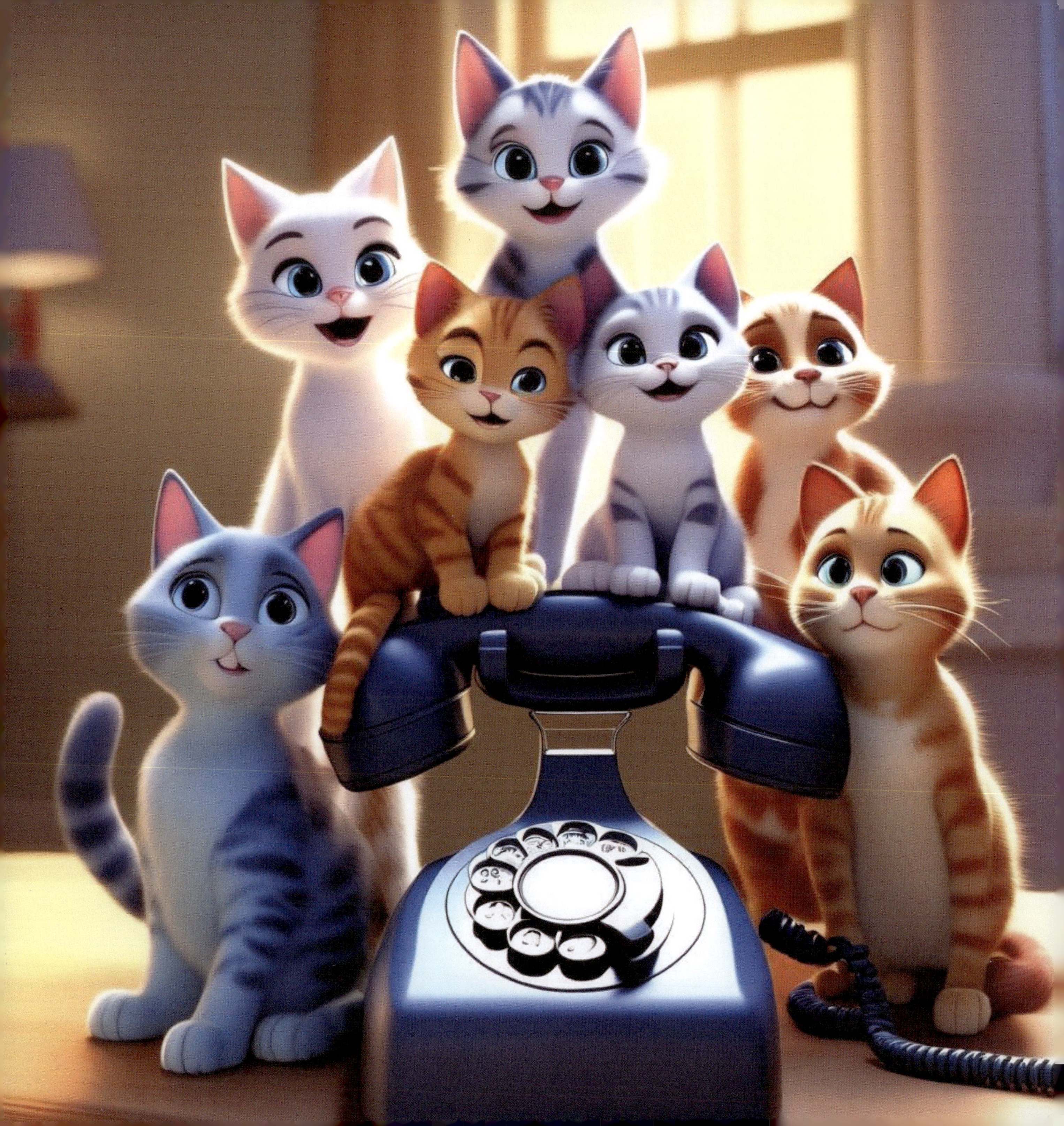

Lily, the melodious cat, would purr in perfect harmony with Freddie's voice.

Oscar, with his mischievous nature, would often tap the phone with his paw, as if he wanted to join in the conversation.

Delilah, with her regal presence, would sit by the phone, listening attentively.

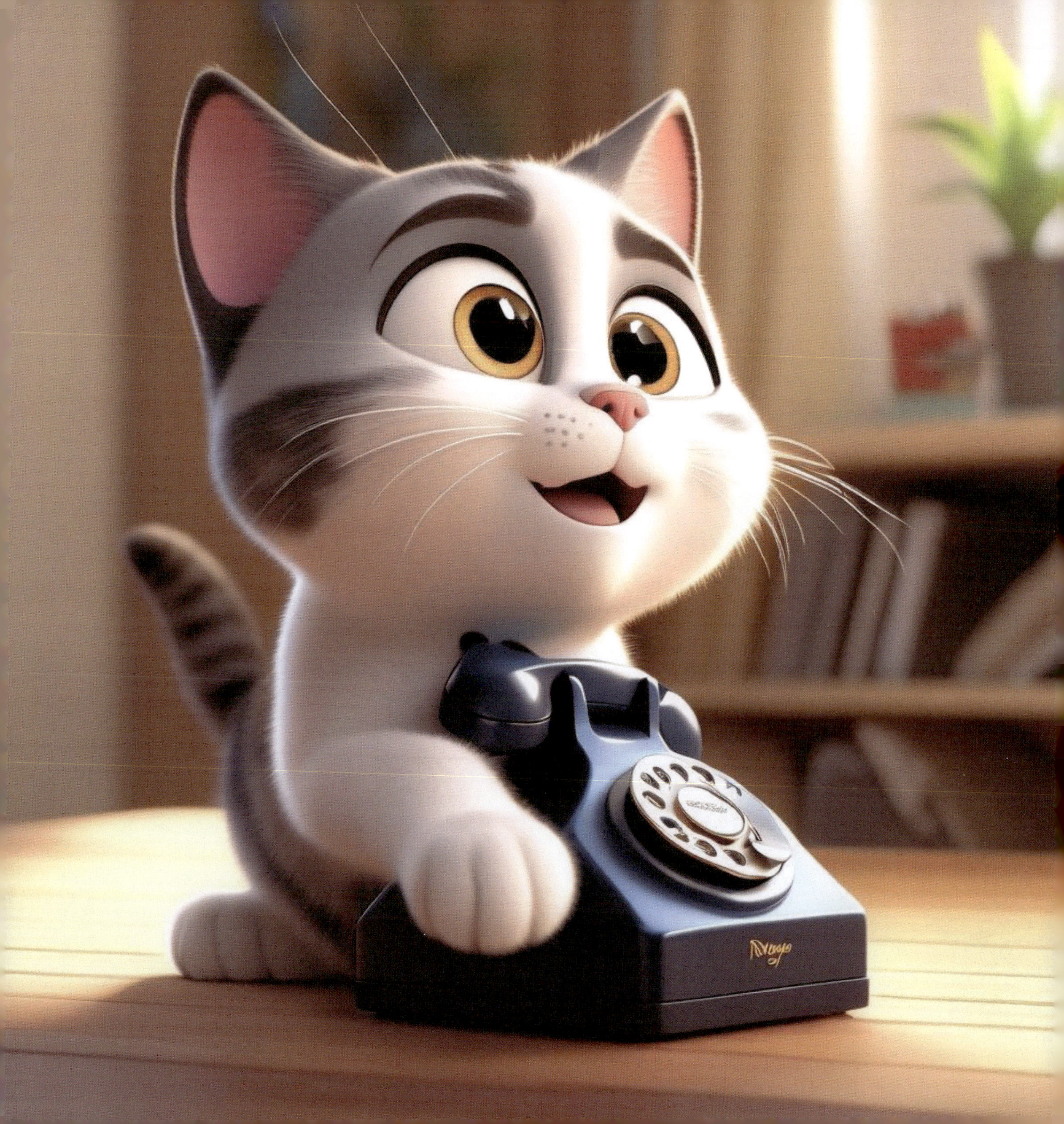

During those magical phone calls, Freddie would tell his cats about the roaring crowds, the dazzling lights, and the magic of music that echoed around the world.

The cats, in turn, would purr tales of their adventures in their cozy cat kingdom.

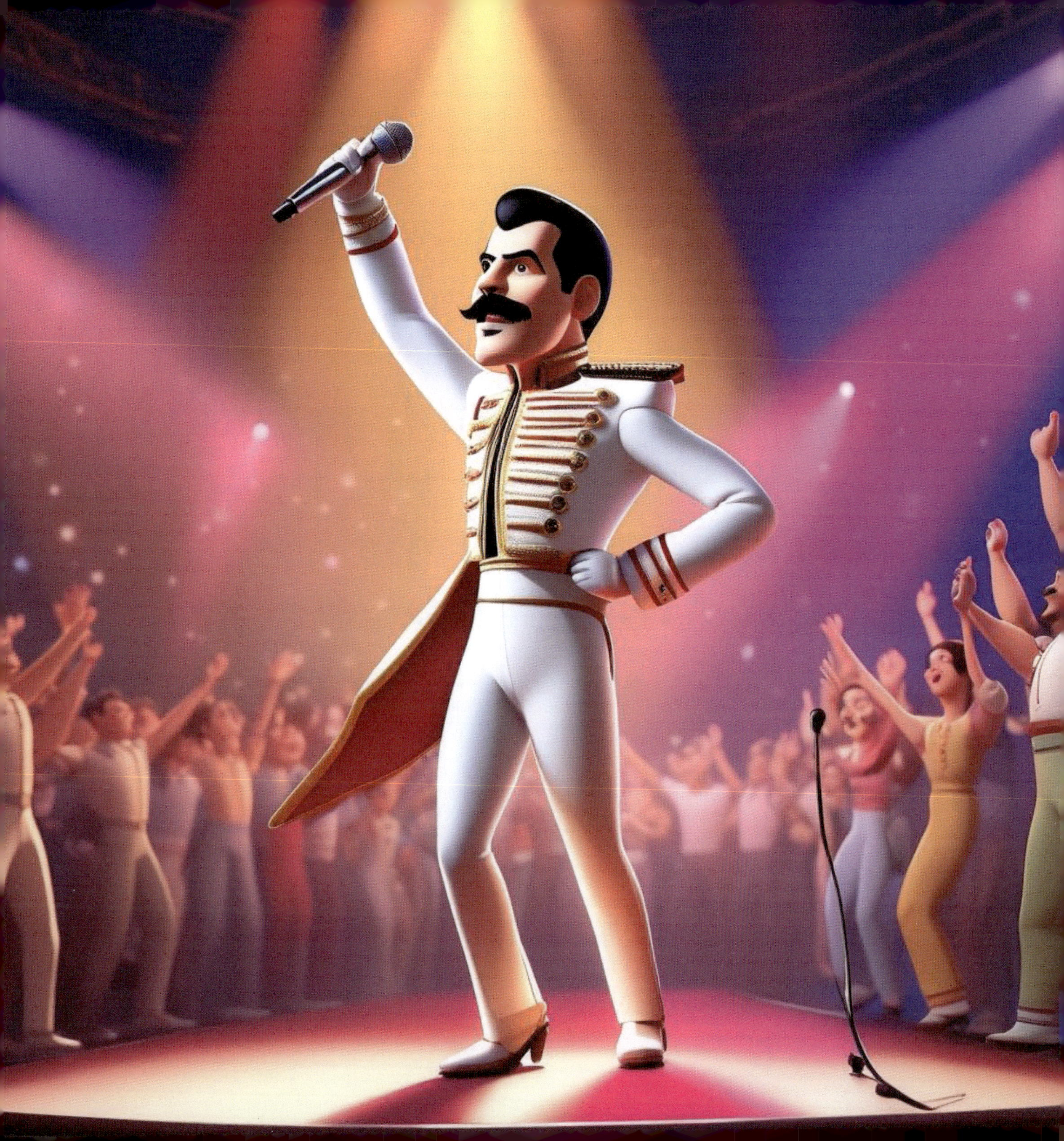

As the tour buses rolled on and the concerts lit up the night, Freddie's heart remained connected to his beloved cats.

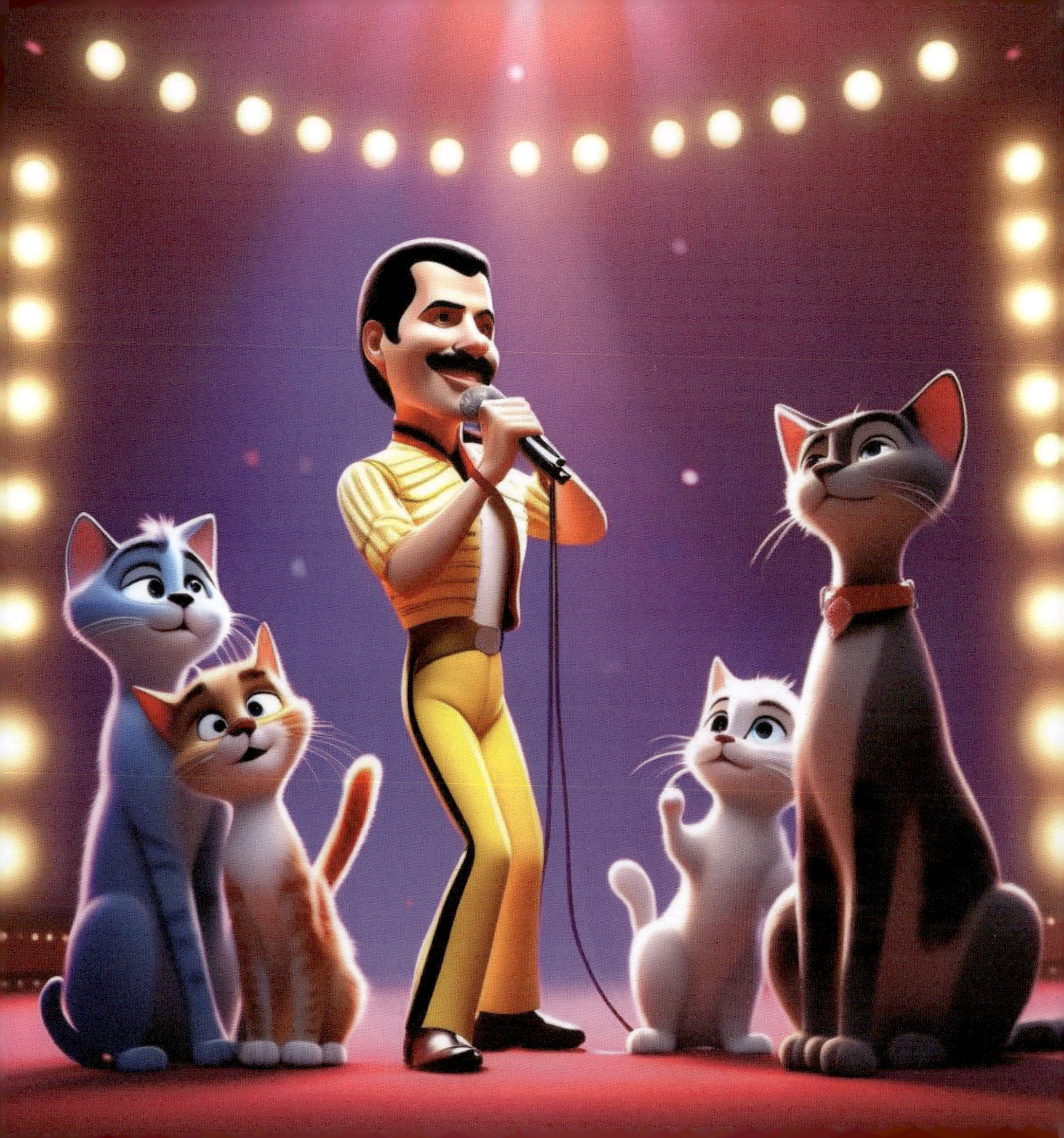

The phone calls became a cherished tradition.

A reminder that no matter how far he travelled, the love for his feline friends always stayed close to his heart.

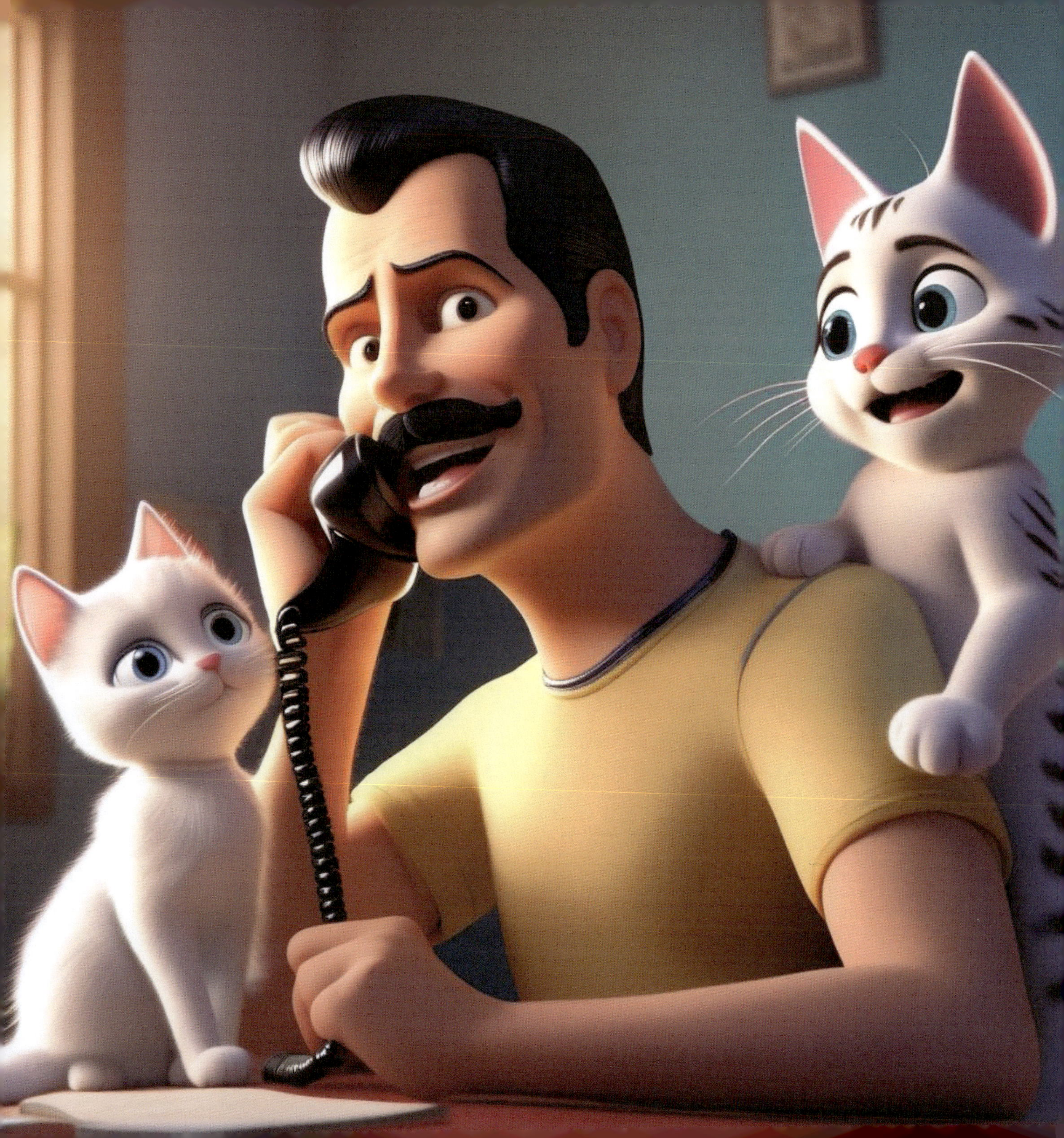

And so, returning home to the town of melodies and meows, Freddie Mercury and his fabulous cats lived happily for many years.

Why? Because they were connected by the magic of music and a love that transcended any distance, even if just a purr away over the phone.

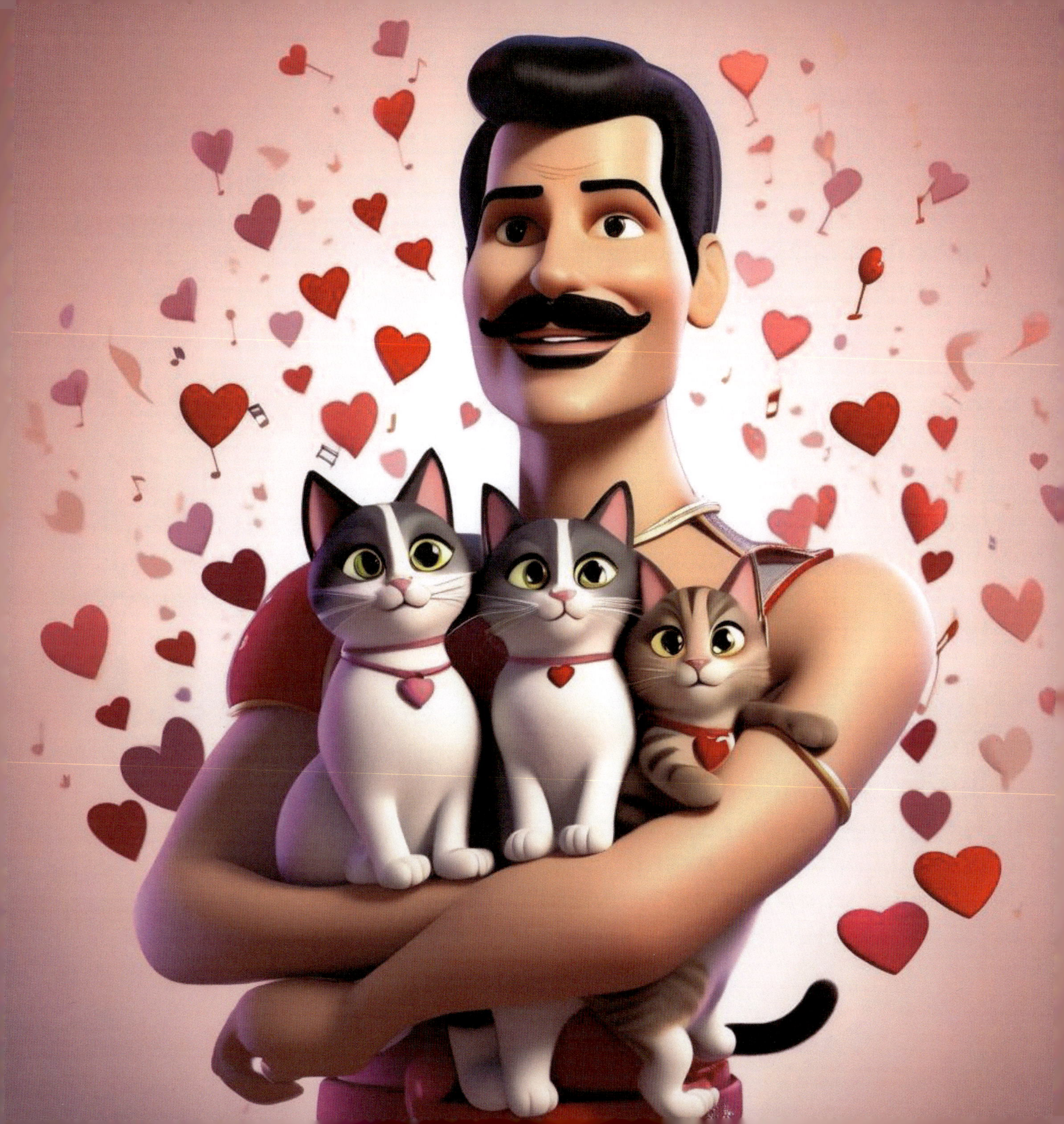

Notes for older readers...

Freddie Mercury, the iconic frontman of the legendary rock band Queen, shared a deep bond with his feline companions. His love for cats was evident in the multiple feline friends that graced his life, with some even making appearances in interviews and photo shoots. Mercury's cats held a special place in his heart, and he often referred to them as his "babies." Notably, his favourite cat, Delilah, even inspired a Queen song of the same name.

Mercury's affection for his cats extended beyond mere companionship; he considered them family. Known for his flamboyant stage presence and powerful vocals, Mercury's softer side emerged in the presence of his beloved cats.

Despite his demanding schedule as a global music icon, Mercury made time for his cherished pets, showcasing a nurturing and compassionate side. His cats brought him solace and comfort, serving as a source of joy in both the highs and lows of his extraordinary life. In celebrating Freddie Mercury, it's not just his musical legacy that endures but also the warmth and love he shared with his furry companions.

Freddie Mercury's deep connection with his cats extended even when he was away on demanding tours. Despite the distances that separated them, Mercury found a unique way to maintain contact with his feline friends. He reportedly phoned his cats while on the road, a testament to the extraordinary lengths he went to, to stay connected with his beloved companions.

This charming detail reveals a softer and more personal side of the rock legend. In the midst of the frenzied world of rock and roll, Mercury's commitment to maintaining a connection with his cats highlights the importance he placed on their presence in his life. It speaks to the profound bond he shared with his furry companions, transcending the boundaries of his demanding career.

These instances of Mercury reaching out to his cats over the phone showcase a heartwarming dimension of his personality, one that goes beyond the stage and studio. It's a touching reminder of the genuine love and care he had for his feline family, adding a delightful and endearing layer to the narrative of Freddie Mercury and his cherished cats.

Author Biography - Meet Kitty and her cats!

Kitty Wilson lives by the sea with her family and cats, Milo, Tillie, George, Agatha, Gabriel, and Margaret.

A life-long cat lover, Kitty spends much of her time working with animal rescue charities to ensure all animals have the life they deserve.

When she isn't working or writing, Kitty loves to entertain her own kitty cats...

Milo, a huge tabby, and 20 years young; Tillie, a Russian blue and spoilt princess; George, a black and white tuxedo cat with a lazy nature; Agatha, a long-haired black cat obsessed with food; and the Tabby Twins, kittens Gabriel and Margaret – tiny terrors who love nothing more than catnip mousies and chasing their older siblings!

Milo

Tillie

George

Agatha

Gabriel and Margaret

Printed in Great Britain
by Amazon